SINGING IN THE NIGHT

SINGING IN THE NIGHT

Collected Meditations, Volume Five

COLLECTED BY
MARY BENARD

SKINNER HOUSE BOOKS
BOSTON

Published by Skinner House Books. Skinner House Books is an imprint of the Unitarian Universalist Association, a liberal religious organization with more than 1,000 congregations in the U.S. and Canada. 25 Beacon Street, Boston, MA 02108-2800.

Printed in Canada

ISBN 1-55896-444-4

Library of Congress Cataloging-in-Publication Data

Singing in the night/collected by Mary Benard
      p.cm.—(Collected meditations; v. 5)
  ISBN 1-55896-444-4 (alk. paper)
    1. Meditations. 2. Unitarian Universalist churches—Prayer-
    books and devotions—English. I. Benard, Mary. II. Series.

BX9855.S57 2004
242—dc22

                              2003070365

5 4 3 2 1
07 06 05 04

The selections included here were previously published by Skinner House Books as follows: *Glory, Hallelujah! Now Please Pick Up Your Socks*, by Jane Ellen Mauldin, 1998; *Dancing in the Empty Spaces*, by David O. Rankin, 2001; *Out of the Ordinary*, by Gordon B. McKeeman, 2000; and *Glad to Be Human*, by Kaaren Solveig Anderson, 2000.

The following meditations were originally published under different titles:
"Singing in the Night" was "Praying."
"Every Minute" was "Common Day."
"Our Common Destiny" was "Talking to Myself."
"We Are Part of the Circle" was "Wakeful Nights."
"How Will We Be Remembered?" was "Ghost."
"The Heart's Geography" was "Healing."
"Your Very Presence" was "Prayer in Action."
"Death Itself" was "Death."

TABLE OF CONTENTS

WE ARE PART OF THE CIRCLE

A TIME TO BE SILENT

In these inspiring meditations faith is not to be taken for granted — it must be attended to, cared for, and practiced. Faith is our work. Gordon McKeeman compares religion to a van that needs regular check-ups, even when you think it's in good working order. These meditations remind us that the divine is incarnate all around us. Kaaren Anderson imagines Eve, banished from the Garden of Eden but thrilled. "I knew it lay before me," Eve exclaims, "my life, my opportunity, my humanness." We can bring Eve's sense of expectation to each new day. And at the end of every day, we can express, with Jane Ellen Mauldin, "a silent sigh of gratitude for yet one more chance to do our job again and go on."

In his poem "Singing in the Night," David Rankin writes, "I love to pray . . . to peek through a mystic window and look upon the fabric of life—how still it breathes, how solemn its march, how profound its perspective . . . and to think how little I know." This deep humility is a hallmark of the four writers represented in this collection—David Rankin, Gordon McKeeman, Kaaren Anderson, and Jane Ellen Mauldin. All four are ministers, but they don't have all the answers. They have convictions and questions. They uphold faith, yet they express honest doubt, inspiring us to become better than we are.

The meditations in this collection have been selected from meditation manuals published every year by the Unitarian Universalist Association. As such, they reflect the theological diversity of Unitarian Universalism, a non-creedal religion that draws inspiration from many faith traditions.

With historical roots in the Jewish and Christian traditions, Unitarian Universalism is a liberal religion —a religion that keeps an open mind to the religious questions people have struggled with in all times and places.

MARY BENARD

SINGING IN THE NIGHT

SINGING IN THE NIGHT

I love to pray, to go deep down into the silence:

>To strip myself of all pride, selfishness, and coldness of heart;

>To peel off thought after thought, passion after passion, till I reach the genuine depths of all;

>To remember how short a time ago I was nothing, and in how short a time again I will not be here;

>To dwell on all joys, all ecstasies, all tender relations that give my life zest and meaning;

>To peek through a mystic window and look upon the fabric of life—how still it breathes, how solemn its march, how profound its perspective;

>And to think how little I know, how very little, except the calm, calm of the silence, and the singing, singing in the night.

Prayer is the soul's intimacy with God, the ultimate kiss.

DAVID O. RANKIN

GYROSCOPE

When I was a child, one of my favorite toys was a gyroscope, a weighty wheel suspended in a cage on an axle. Winding a string around the axle and pulling the string would start the wheel spinning rapidly. When the wheel was spinning, the gyroscope resisted efforts to change its position. It could be perched precariously on a sharp edge or on a length of string and maintain its position. Later, I discovered that gyroscopes had other, more important functions than entertaining children. Keeping ships at sea on an even keel was one of them.

Still later, when I was an active parish minister, someone once described my style of ministry as gyroscopic. I gathered that this person noticed that I tried to keep the church on an even keel and moving forward by trying continuously to balance the emphases of the church's programs: stressing social responsibility when we were very busy with personal faith issues and reminding members of personal religious disciplines when we were absorbed in social action.

Now I'm very much occupied with maintaining my own personal equilibrium. This is true physically. I try hard not to fall. Older folks are often seriously injured in falls. But there's much more to it. I also have diabetes, and blood glucose control is an important health measure. In this area, again, balance is important. I also try to keep abreast of current events, a field in which equilibrium is seriously challenged because of the turbulence of our times. Probably you cherish equilibrium, too, for reasons similar to mine.

The most intriguing aspect of the gyroscope is that it works by spinning rapidly. This rapid rotation in a fixed location creates resistance to moving away from that plane. If the wheel ceases spinning, its resistance vanishes and it is easily moved to any position.

It occurs to me that my religious faith, the wheel of core convictions in my life, has to be moving continuously if I am to keep my balance, mentally and spiritually. Friction and gravity operate to slow down the gyroscope's wheel. Likewise, if I do not keep my faith going steadily, it may well lose its ability to keep me on an even keel, thereby protecting me from being overwhelmed, capsized by the turmoil and tumult around me. A regular pause in the day's course to check my gyroscope is important to me. You never know when some gale, hurricane, crisis, or tragedy will begin beating on your equilibrium, your peace of mind, your composure. Check your gyroscope. Make sure it's spinning serenely around your axle's fixed points.

GORDON B. McKEEMAN

BELIEVING

I believe in the Holy,
    lifting, sustaining,
    among us, within us,
    around us.

I believe in Living,
    with a song to sing,
    in awe, in adoration,
    out of joy, out of praise.

I believe in Loving,
    in intimate communion,
    of gentle compassion,
    and the giving of roses.

I believe in Seeking,
    daring to explore,
    doubting without fear,
    cautious in certainties.

I believe in Prophecy,
    the spirit of outrage,
    clapping like thunder,
    healing the world.

DAVID O. RANKIN

THE SPIRITUAL JOURNEY

In the pulpit, I cannot preach bromides: If it is easy, it is probably false; if it is popular, it is soon outmoded; if it is soothing, it is lacking depth; if it is final, it is clearly dead—and what remains is the rigorous journey, which demands the highest degree of dogged persistence.

It is Moses leading the Jews through the desert of Sinai, and Jesus enduring the temptations in the wilderness of Israel, and Buddha seeking enlightenment along the dusty roads of India.

It is the glorious voyage of Odysseus in Homer's *Odyssey*, the narrow paths through the circles of hell in Dante's *Inferno*, and the confessions of the travelers in Chaucer's *Canterbury Tales*.

It is the pilgrims sailing on the Mayflower, the settlers moving westward, being *On the Road* with Jack Kerouac, and spinning through a black hole in Kubrick's *2001: A Space Odyssey*.

Whatever the specific goal: a battle for honor, a ritual of passage, a quest for the grail, a return to Eden, a search for identity, a pilgrimage to Mecca, or a visit to the land of Oz, there is always the higher journey toward spiritual fulfillment—of rebirth, renewal, and transfiguration.

DAVID O. RANKIN

FALLING OUT OF BED

Very early a few mornings ago, I fell out of bed. It was not—I repeat *not*—an ordinary event. I don't recall ever having done so before. And I hope I'll not do it again. Apparently, as I slipped over the edge, I made a desperate grab for something firm to prevent my fall. The night table wasn't it. It tipped, drawers slid out, and I bruised a knee on the corner of a drawer. It hurt. I was very uncomfortable, not a little chagrined, puzzled, a bit angry, and (need I say) unhappy. How did it happen? I didn't know. I wasn't en route to anywhere. I wasn't even awake until I began to fall.

Then I thought of a little squib from a church newsletter of at least a generation ago: "People fall out of church for the same reason that children fall out of bed: they fall asleep too near the place where they get in." That's the reason. I fell asleep too near the place where I got in. End of story? Not really. I began to wonder whether such accidents happen in other contexts.

There are many, many books that remain unread. I went to sleep too near the place where I got in. And there are many people I might have gotten to know better, listened more intently and purposefully to their stories rather than waiting for a pause so I could tell mine. I went to sleep too near the edge.

I hear people talking about "living on the edge"—I suppose at the boundary between the known and the unknown. In some sense, we all dwell in that realm. Each new dawn heralds an unknown day. We sometimes assure ourselves that the new one will be similar to those we have already lived. We feel reassured by the hope of reliability.

My unexpected, disorienting, and discomforting fall out of bed has impressed upon me the conviction that the edge is not a good place to fall asleep. If you go to sleep there, you're likely to miss some great new happenings, like the ending of a conflict, a truce between old enemies, a new bit of community taking root in a casual acquaintanceship, or a new blossom sprung from an old plant. Of course, we must sleep. I can tell you it's not a good idea to go to sleep too near the place where you get in. The edge is an all right place, but it's not for sleeping.

GORDON B. McKEEMAN

DEAD BATTERY

Our camper van is one of the less active members of the family. It does a great deal of they-also-serve-who-only-stand-and-wait duty. It's reassuring to see the van there ready to burst into activity at the turn of its key, admirably alert for a vacation jaunt or a bulky load that would overwhelm our modest sedan. The other day, though, when our constant-duty vehicle was absent on errands, I needed to undertake what seemed an urgent mission. So I took to the van and turned the key. Nothing. Not a cough. Not a tremor. Not a flickering light. Nothing. My routine and instantaneous diagnosis: a dead battery. The battery was five years old, and it had probably died a slow death because of prolonged inactivity aided by the subtle and gradual drain of an unturned-off radio.

Once the local AAA service came and jolted the engine into unaccustomed action, a new battery was obtained and installed, and the faithful van was rehabilitated for further action-ready, patient waiting. It occurred to me that sometimes we leave our religions sitting idly in the corners of our lives awaiting some emergency—a crisis, accident, or untoward happening. Day by day, however, the depredations of our time have drained away our religion's power. Comes a crisis, we leap to our religion and turn the key. Not a whimper, a cough, or a shudder. No light flickers. Nothing.

Then we are reminded that a little preventive maintenance might have kept our faith energized for just such a time as this. That's one of the reasons that even a simple daily devotional practice and/or regular attendance at communal worship needs to be a part of our ordinary routine—it keeps one's religion in working order. It's no accident that my automobile mechanic suggests a weekly running of the van. Likewise, religious institutions offer weekly opportunities for the worshipful gathering of the faithful. It's to keep our religion in good shape.

We never know when an urgent need for our deep and active faith will arise. So it's a good idea to keep it in good shape. It's sad to see people who thought they had an active faith discover that it has lost its resilience through prolonged disuse. It looked strong as it sat there, but it had a dead battery. When people ask why I attend church so regularly, I respond, "I go to church to recharge my battery." I want to be as sure as I can that my religion will be ready to serve when it is most urgently needed.

GORDON B. McKEEMAN

DAMP AND OOZY

It's another rainy morning at the doctor's office. I sit, over-stimulated and waiting, my head full of the crud that brought me here. My young children cough enticingly into my face ("Here, Mom, if you don't have enough germs already, you can share mine!").

I do not like to wait. I prefer to be going, running, driving, typing, *accomplishing*, for Pete's sake. Yet here I sit, waiting.

I assume there is a lesson somewhere in my visits here. You know the lesson. You could write it yourself: "Be here now. Live for the moment. Relax." I'm certainly much better at preaching it than living it. Right now, as I sneeze, blow, and wipe runny noses, I would rather not be here at all, lesson or no lesson.

Jesus is reported to have said, "Split the wood and you shall find me. Lift the stone and there I am." In other words, the holiness of life can be found in damp, moist, oozy, natural places, too. Well, my family has damp, moist, and oozy down pretty well. The holy, huh? Right here, huh?

Perhaps this is a test. It's much easier to see the holy revealed in the stars at night, or in the glory of a great choral "Hallelujah!" But here, in a moment filled with waiting-room noise, diaper bags, and sinus headaches, if I can find it, it oughta be easy the rest of the time.

JANE ELLEN MAULDIN

MY WORLD

My world? Not so.

I may be the world's
but the only part of it that is mine is that private
interior view I have of events, places, and people
the world filtered through my feeling, my hope
and, sometimes, my despair.

Its light and shadows are my knowledge and ignorance
Its height and depths are the geography of my soul
Its rain, my tears; its sunshine, my laughter.

I long sometimes to escape the prison of my being
to see things as they are
    and then I wonder if I am not safer
    in my own interior world, where facts
    can be molded and reality shaped to
    my own needs.

So, in the end, I safely enfold myself in my own
world chrysalis.

But, now and then
a shaft of out-there penetrates the in-here
    sometimes it is a wound
    sometimes a freshening breeze
    sometimes a hearth-brightening blaze
    or a flash of light illumining for an instant
        the darkness of my self-prison.

Arise, prisoner in your dungeon-self!
    Tear away the bars
    Crumble away the concrete
    Melt the locks.

Trust yourself to the world.
It will possess you in the end.
    Let it have you living
    That it may cradle you dead.

GORDON B. MCKEEMAN

GRATITUDE CIRCLE

We've begun a new ritual around our dinner table in which each member of the family takes a minute or two to name what he or she is grateful for. No matter how yucky our day has been, we try to offer our gratitude in a spirit of kindness and real thankfulness. Often, the ritual's nicest effect is to calm the troops who may be feeling a bit rowdy or punchy. That's on a good evening. Other times, well . . .

"Today," said I one evening, trying to model appropriate behavior (usually a ludicrous pursuit), "I am thankful for the wonderful rain we had this afternoon, which watered all the trees and grass and flowers so they can grow."

"Today," said Daughter #1, "I am grateful for the rain and the trees and the flowers. And I am grateful for Mom and Dad and Sister and Brother and Dog." (A not-so-subtle attempt at ingratiating herself, as her sly smile implied, but spoken with heartfelt emotion, nonetheless.)

"Today," said Daughter #2, "I am grateful for Mom and Dad and Brother and Dog." A smirk.

"What?" Dad and Mom were stunned. "What about your sister?" Daughter #1 immediately recognized the implications of Daughter #2's statement, which pointedly left her out. She burst into tears and ran from the table.

We continue to work on gratitude circles at our house. Some of us find it hard to be thankful when we would rather be angry. Sometimes even I (who like to consider myself closer to perfect than many) would rather give my husband a swift verbal kick than words of appreciation.

Yet, there is something sacred about our gratitude circles. Gratitude has a healing power at our table that is more tangible than forgiveness or even ice cream. We can't honestly nourish a grudge at the same time that we nourish gratitude.

So we try. Daughter #1 came back to the table and we talked about forgiveness as well as gratitude, and we wondered aloud about pain and healing in words a child might be able to fathom.

And we grown-ups gave a silent sigh of gratitude for yet one more chance to do our job again and go on.

JANE ELLEN MAULDIN

PRAYER FOR FAITH

So often words fail us
And we do not know to whom or what to pray.

We ask for legs that can walk for peace,
Arms that can work for justice,
Voices that can speak with love,
Hands that can soothe a feverish brow.

By our actions and voices
May our prayers be sent.

Shalom. Salaam. Om. Amen.

JANE ELLEN MAULDIN

THE MEEK INHERIT THE EARTH

Lucille was a long-time member of the church, an extremely shy and humble individual. When I visited her at the hospital, I learned she was suffering from leukemia. We talked for a short time, although she was very weak.

As I tiptoed from the room, she said in a soft voice, "I have not completed my pledge to the church." Surprised by the comment, I replied, "Don't you worry. It can certainly wait. I'll see you in the morning." She died that night.

But sometime during the evening hours, between the moment I left the room and the moment she died, Lucille had managed to get out of bed. She made her way to a dresser in the corner of the room. She found a pen and a checkbook.

With a shaking hand, she wrote a check to the church she loved for many years. I found it in the mail the day after her death, the last communication of a tidy soul. It was the most memorable pledge I have ever received.

DAVID O. RANKIN

NATURAL THEOLOGY

Is there such a thing as God?

I saw a sunrise at Jackson Hole.

I fell in love many years ago.

I caught a tear in my father's eye.

I watched a lily bloom.

I saved a boy from drugs and death.

I touched the hand of Martin Luther King, Jr.

I feel the warmth of children.

I laugh almost every day.

I hold the hem of hope.

The only God I can possibly know is the God of life—
and life is endless.

DAVID O. RANKIN

EVERY MINUTE

EVERY MINUTE

A decade ago Japanese Emperor Hirohito died.
There was much speculation about his role in World
War II. I wondered then, and I wonder occasionally
even now, what his life must have been like. He did
not choose to be Emperor; it was an accident of
birth, a hereditary position. All accounts of his life
describe him as retiring and shy, most at home in
a biological laboratory studying various marine
species. He wrote several books on the subject.
As Emperor he had little actual power and enormous
symbolic power. He took actual power only once, after
the dropping of atomic bombs on Hiroshima and
Nagasaki. When Japan's military leaders disagreed
about continuing the war, he decreed a surrender.
He said once that his fondest dream was to live just
one day as a common person. His fondest dream!

Most of us live the Emperor's dream day after day.
It may never occur to us that we are the daily recipi-
ents of what the Emperor could only vainly hope to
have: a day as a common person. A common day
replete with common things, the kinds of things we
take so for granted:

> sleeping and waking again to a new day

> performing simple chores: dressing, making the
> bed, eating breakfast

reading (or seeing) the world's new terrors and torments, tragedies, and triumphs

doing ordinary work, whose impact is largely unfathomable but would be missed by someone if it were not done: the laundry, cleaning, meal preparation

looking out upon the ordinary world, breathing the air, drinking the water, enjoying children at play, marveling at the beauty of flowers, the vastness of the sky, the gutsy heroism of simple folk

remembering loved ones near and far: those who have been our teachers; our companions and acquaintances; our benefactors and beneficiaries; our neighbors, even our ancestors, who lived through common days, mostly hard, and occasionally tolerable or easy

calling to mind those who bequeath color, fragrance, and texture to each common day

recalling the vast fabric of love and labor performed day and night by those unknown to us, who make our lives easier

and a thousand more unmentioned blessings.

One who finds so many wonders and beneficences in a common day understands deeply the line uttered by Emily in Thornton Wilder's *Our*

Town: "Oh, earth, you're too wonderful for anybody to realize you," followed by the anguished question, "Do any human beings ever realize life while they live it—every, every minute?"

Today is one common day, one (more) chance to be fully alive. Welcome to it!

GORDON B. McKEEMAN

EVE'S MUSE

Describe Adam, you say. Well, he's kind of a wuss. Don't get me wrong, though, Adam's a nice guy. He just adheres to rules a little too strictly. Take his conversation with God before I was created. God tells my husband not to eat fruit from a tree in the center of the garden. Adam unquestioningly goes along with the deal, "Sure God, I won't ever, ever touch that tree's fruit, cross my heart, hope to die."

That's Adam, just hanging out and enjoying this "paradise" as he calls it. Well, let me tell you, paradise wasn't nirvana. It was beautiful: luscious lakes, meandering rivers, verdant trees, prolific flowers, stunning mountains, but . . . boring. The Garden of Eden lost its appeal pretty quickly. It was nice not to have to work. It was nice essentially to have God wait on you hand and foot. Food was abundant, scenery ever wonderful, seventy degree days, light showers in the afternoon, and then back to perfect.

But, have you ever longed for something because life felt like a matzah cracker—dry and thin? Have you ever wanted something because you knew it would add spontaneity, diversity, and just plain change to your life? I did. Life sat pathetically before me on a silver platter. I didn't have to work, struggle, worry, engage, or contemplate. Life was supposedly perfect, and I was bored. Personally, I think God was bored too. Why else set up something to tempt so blatantly?

God also knew me. He knew I couldn't be stopped. He saw me bored out of my mind in that garden. Adam and I used to sit idly around, waiting for something to happen, anything to happen. I fell to twiddling my thumbs. Adam used to ask, "Is that all you know how to do?"

I'd tell him, "No, I can go this way too" and change the direction of my thumb twiddling. It got to the point where death didn't seem like such a bad alternative to boredom. At least monotony would get a run for its money.

Enter the snake. Smooth voice, pleasant serpent smile. A reptile that made sense. The snake reminded me that it was God who told Adam not to eat the apple. I was getting all my information secondhand.

"Remember," the snake reminded me, "Adam would rather stay in this so-called paradise with the same day, day after day, than to risk, or challenge, or imagine, or venture anything."

It was then that I looked into those snake's eyes and I saw my life. In great big capital letters, the irises of that snake read, boring. I saw myself and myself saw me. It was then that I knew I had to taste that apple. So, I did. I took a bite of that tart crispness. And all felt different. My body changed. I felt the sores on my feet. I felt a surge of life in my belly, my mind expand, my vision clear. For the first time, I felt whole. The spirit of life and love had consumed me. I felt wholly alive. Full of the spirit of God. So, I went to find Adam. I tried to explain how I felt. He just looked at me in horror and amazement, yet he kept asking me what it felt like. All I could think to say was, "I'm truly human. Adam, I feel more me than ever before!" I cajoled, argued, and finally just gave up. I shoved the apple into his taut mouth. He reluctantly took a bite. It was later that he told God it was all my fault.

Now here is the part of the story that I must confess needs correcting. I didn't blame the snake for my transgressions. I fessed up and admitted I had eaten the apple. I said in a proud, unwavering voice to God, "I am glad to be human! I can spurtle with rage, shake with despair, and bubble in ecstasy. Everything is not perfect, but it is real, alive! I feel sorry for you, God. For you everything is perfect, always going your way. Do you ever get bored? Want to be alive like me?"

Then God got mad. He cursed us both. He said that I would scream out in pain during childbirth, that I would regret the day I was born. But I must say, I never expected anything different after watching the animals in the garden give birth. They too suffered pain, yet had such a magnificent way to appreciate the outcome. We listened to the end of his tirade, and Adam just plopped down right there, looking out at everything he felt he had lost.

I picked up the apple and went to the gate. I stood there for a while, leaning against that cold wrought iron, throwing the apple up and down. Up and down. Up and down. I stood enjoying the rhythm of that apple slap into my hand, followed by silence as the air embraced it for a brief moment. Then slap. Then rest. Then slap. I looked out over the vast expanse of that wilderness, thinking about a song I had heard, "You can make the world your apple, take a bite before it sours, you can make the world your charm or your chain." I knew it lay before me, my life, my opportunity, my humanness. And I said out loud, in a clear voice, "I'm so glad to be human!"

KAAREN SOLVEIG ANDERSON

DING-A-LING-A-LING!

When I was a child, the day after Thanksgiving was steeped in ritual. Every year my family would travel to Chicago for the holiday festivities. Our tour was always the same: We'd tromp up and down Michigan Ave., admiring store windows with animated mechanical dolls that served as actors for the narrated holiday story. We would wait in line for two hours to sit under the three-story tree at Marshall Fields and enjoy a formal lunch, and sit on Santa's lap to discuss the finer points of our list. Then on to the Berghoff for dinner.

The day always held magic, mostly because of my dime-laden mittens. In the morning, my dad would give my sister and me each a handful of dimes, which I kept in my mittens so I could tinker with them as we walked in anticipation of finding another one of "them"—Salvation Army Christmas buckets. At almost every corner familiar red cans awaited. I marveled in watching my dimes swirl their way to the quarter-sized slot and plunk in to rest amid other dime-sized donations. At the time, I knew nothing about Salvation Army theology, only that they worked for the homeless and destitute. They became my symbol of generosity for the season, albeit bucket-sized.

As an adult, I often felt an odd pull to ring the bell myself. One year I gave in. I called up the lieutenant at the local Salvation Army and asked enthusiastically if they were in need of help. They were. I was given two assignments. I couldn't wait to get my hands on that little tinkly bell.

The first assignment was a busy street corner with a bookstore and coffee shop on either side. I rang my ding-a-lingy bell in ten-degree weather with glee, stamping my feet periodically to stay warm. My smart bucket swung slightly in the breeze. It was an experience just as I had hoped: people asked me if I was warm enough, a couple bought me coffee, many smiled and simply wished me "Happy Holidays" as they passed. I marveled at the parade of dime donors and the familiar "plunk" of change that followed.

The second assignment was at a mall across from JC Penney's. Once again eager, I itched to start my ring-a-dinging. The lieutenant arrived to set up my bucket. My hands reached for the bell. No bell. He explained, "The mall owners have complained, no bells, only this." He handed me a sign.

The sign was attached to a long dowel. On the top of the dowel, two pieces of paper were stapled together over the center of the stick. One side read "DING," the other "DONG." Instead of ringing, I now had to flip a sign that read "DING-DONG." My little bucket instantly lost its ting-a-ling. My enthusiasm waned. I flipped in silent motion. It seemed absurd, but I went to work. People pushed past each other, mired in that Christmas hubbub that leans toward frustration, not joy. Then they'd spot me. Their faces would contort, scrunching up into laughter and that uncomfortable feeling when you're embarrassed and humored by someone at the same time. They would often throw in some dimes and say "Happy Holidays," barely able to stifle an awkward yet justifiable smirk. I fought hard not to feel like the sign was projecting my mental state to the mall community.

For four hours I flipped—the sign, that is. Ten minutes before I was to quit, this fellow in black cowboy boots and a ten-gallon hat walked up to me and laughed. He was full out chuckles, bent over, hysterically laughing. I stood taller, flipping my sign with increased vigor. I couldn't tell where he was going with this. When he finally stood up for air, his eyes were smiling, so I hoped for no malicious intent. But I also was ready to kick him in the shins for his reaction to me and my now stupid sign.

Then he said, "I must say, I've never seen a sign like that before. Anybody that stands with a sign that says 'Ding-Dong' must be duly rewarded." He reached into his back pocket and retrieved his wallet. Crisp bills lay neatly in uniform order. He ran through the fives, tens, and twenties, and got to a row of fifties. He pulled one out. A fifty. He neatly folded the bill and squeezed it into the bucket designed for coin donors. Nodding, he smiled right into my eyes and muttered, "Well, I never." Then he continued on through the mall with laughter that hung captive in the air like lingering pipe smoke.

I, on the other hand, began to turn that sign with a renewed vigor. I looked at each passerby with a new attitude, whether they snickered or smiled, donated or not. I now felt strangely in awe of my DING-DONG sign. I was unabashedly proud that I was stupid enough to stand in a mall tenaciously flipping a sign, waiting for humor and generosity to awaken someone's humdrum spirit. Waiting for it to finally dawn on me that my gifts of generosity and time needed to lose their pretenses in order for any true generosity to occur. Waiting, just to discover, that this season can still thrill and surprise. Waiting for magic, only to find that red buckets held it all the time. Even without the ding-a-ling.

KAAREN SOLVEIG ANDERSON

NOT DYING

I once thought that I was going to die. Not just in-the-future-it-happens-to-all-of-us-because-we-are-mortal die, but *die now*. I didn't die, but I learned a little humility along the way.

My husband and I were coming home from our first adults-only vacation in years. As I was pregnant with our third child, we also knew that it would be our last adults-only vacation for a long time to come.

Approaching home, the plane flew through terrible storms. I have flown many times in bad weather, but this was different. Thunder roared around us without ceasing; the plane tossed and fell like a bird in a tornado. As the storm mounted in intensity, I began to focus not on what might go right, but on what might go wrong. I remembered how unorganized people and procedures had been earlier at the airport. I remembered the youth of the pilots.

Then I remembered one more thing: An old woman had read my palm at a wedding years ago and had remarked purposefully that I would have two children and would die young. My memory of this very suspicious, unscientific statement, thrown into the brew of my observations about the airline and the storm, and mixed with a good dose of pregnancy hormones resulted in the obvious conclusion: We were all going to die.

I prepared myself for the end. First, I told Harry I loved him. (He looked at me kindly and patted me on the knee.) Next, I thought of how my children would respond to the news of our deaths. I cried as I thought of their grief and pain. I knew that they would be raised by loving family members. They would be all right.

Then, I turned to the serious business at hand. I focused my concentration on the light that I thought was sure to come. Would there be a long, dark tunnel with a blazing sun at the end? Would there be a rebirth somehow? I did not know the answers. All that seemed important was to feel peaceful, calm, and loving. That attitude, felt deep in my heart, seemed to be the most appropriate way to meet death.

And then the plane broke through the clouds. It had stopped twisting and churning and headed straight for the runway. As we touched down, a loud cheer erupted throughout the aircraft. We were down. We were safe. We were not going to die at this time. I broke into sobs, shaking with the intensity of my experience.

A few minutes later, as we were preparing to get off the plane, I found myself perturbed with the clumsy people ahead of me. I complained testily to Harry. He looked at me quietly. "You don't sound like someone who just thought she was going to die." Then I remembered the attitude of love for everyone and everything that I felt was the way to meet death. Surely it is the best way to meet life, too. If I could maintain that focus, I would be ready for every moment, whatever that moment would bring. I can't do it all the time—it's difficult to do it even some of the time—but it's worth a try.

JANE ELLEN MAULDIN

PLACES, PLACES, PLEASE!

In December I journey to Chicago to perform the wedding of one of my best friends, an actress of striking good looks and commanding confidence. She has a strong presence, a dancer's long stride, and perfect posture. I stand with hips out and have a slouchy walk. I am four inches taller than she is, but I often feel shorter. We make a great pair.

At the rehearsal, I realize that I am the only one in the wedding party who is not a professional actor. And I don't mean actors as in I-wait-tables-and-call-myself-an-actor actors. These are working actors: six Broadway actors, one soap opera star, and a movie and sitcom actress. I am in the company of true thespians.

The hubbub starts. Groomsmen call out, "Places, places, please." Bridesmaids admonish, "Quiet on the set." The bride and groom stomp around, clapping their hands and exclaiming, "Let's go people, chop, chop!" I, the one who is supposed to be running the show, am being manipulated, manhandled, and upstaged! After the places and blocking, the run-through begins with what they call the overture, a medley of show tunes. People move to their marks, walk in practiced step down the stairs, and read their words with resonant tone and measured speech. I don't utter a word. I never get the chance. There is stiff competition for my role. In the end, I mumble,

"This is supposed to be a spiritual event folks, not an audition." I am a director without direction.

Next day, wedding day, I arrive at the house and go upstairs to find my friend. The room is filled with women in their twenties and thirties in drop-dead outfits. This company of decked-to-the-hilt modelettes surely required the aid of butter knives to enter their dresses. My friend's wedding dress, a cream satin, complete with opera gloves, was designed by the costume designer on her recent tour. She looks stunning, as all brides do. Dressed for my role as minister in a demure blue suit, I am feeling frumpier by the minute.

I go downstairs and stroll casually through the assembling congregation. The hairdresser and his wares monopolize the dining room table. His shoulder-length hair is feathered and lacquered solid like a seventies country singer. His assistant's hands are a riot of rhinestones and gold, and chime as he swiftly hands combs and brushes. One large guest in her (his?) sixties is standing next to me in a long black sequin gown, an eight-foot black feather boa draped exotically over her shoulders, and three-inch eyelashes splashed with silver glitter. Then the women in their seventies arrive, all wearing skirts that leave nothing to the imagination. The grand-mother of the groom is most memorable: miniskirt, bright red stockings, black stiletto heels, and a vampish cigarette holder. (If my legs happen to be that shapely when I'm seventy, forgive me if the navy suit hangs unused in my closet. The heads can turn to me, officiating minister.)

The wedding starts. Show tunes call everyone to their places. The mothers walk down the elegant staircase, gowns dancing in time to the music. Then my friend enters, looking radiant. Everyone is in place. There is quiet on the set. I start the ceremony.

The wedding is very emotional. My friend and her partner say their vows to one another with great vigor and intention. They both start sniffling. Then the soap opera star launches into Shakespearean monologue. Drama fills the air. My friend's soon-to-be husband shivers with emotion. Tears don't trickle lightly from his eyes; they cascade. He is in need of a rain gutter. The soap opera star joins in. It occurs to me that either they are exceptional actors or they are deeply moved. I opt for the latter. I myself start to lose my composure, my eyes pooling. The soap opera star stops mid-sentence to gather himself. The room is filled with sniveling, quiet snorts, and sharp, in-drawn breaths.

A video camera is pointed directly at me, capturing each precious moment on tape. My eyes are teary and red, my make-up smeared. By this time, the glamor is gone. And my nose is running. Dripping on my stole, I ask myself how I'm feeling, "Humbled? Humiliated? Raw?"

I am not alone. There is no pretense left. No superficiality. There is a new camaraderie between stranger and friend, as tissues are passed from one hand to another. Surprised by our own humility, by our own vulnerable selves, exposed so severely to one another, we are privileged to witness a simple act—love shared and given. And at that moment, it doesn't matter that these are professionals, that everyone makes their cues, or that the costumes are beautiful. What matters is two naked souls, expressing the love that makes the world move. I stand aside following the service and let myself feel the full spin of the earth, moving quicker in that moment, and smile.

KAAREN SOLVEIG ANDERSON

WHAT THE CHICKEN TAUGHT

I dislike harming any animal, even ants, so killing our chicken was not how I had planned to spend the morning.

This was a rather special chicken, as chickens go. Beloved friends gave us four chickens a while back, but some varmint came out of the woods and got three of them right away. This chicken, however, had the wit to survive. She also had a grain of defiance.

She wouldn't stay caged in a safe pen. Every morning, she flew over the pen fence and spent the day pecking around the yard. I liked her, I liked her defiance, and she seemed to like us. She often came up the eight steps onto our back porch and poked around, leaving her droppings (which I didn't like) as reminders of her chickenness. Some evenings we were able to entice her back inside the pen, but other times, including last night, she continued to roam. Her freedom was her downfall.

We found her by the back porch steps this morning. She looked at us calmly, eyes blinking. The entire back part of her body had been ripped open by some creature with claws. Harry and I knew what we had to do. We loaded the kids into the car and I backed the car out of the yard while he took the shovel blade to the chicken. After Harry got in the car and drove away to run errands, I walked back alone to perform the burial and found her still alive, breathing and looking at me. I did what I had to do, cursing, crying, and praying simultaneously.

"Please die, chicken. Please die!"

"I'm sorry, chicken. I'm sorry!"

Chickens are hard to kill. I am basically a city kid and did not know this, remembering only the story of my great-grandmother who could wring a chicken's neck with one twist. My chicken didn't die that way. After it was all over, I buried her at the edge of the woods.

Today I am shaken and sad. How far I have come from my great-grandmother's time of relying on home gardens and home chickens for food and survival. How far I have come from being part of the everyday cycles of life and death. I feel as if I have forgotten some basic knowledge.

Life is more simple and fleeting than I like to pretend. I am feeling very animal now, flesh and blood, breath and fur, aware of the transience of my animal body. That chicken clung to life fiercely. But in the end, she was delicate bones that broke. My bones feel more frail today. My breath feels quicker. I am awed by how fragile and fleeting and extremely precious life is.

Thank you, chicken. Thank you.

JANE ELLEN MAULDIN

ZAINE'S FAIRY WINGS

Four years ago, I moved to a small town from New York City. At first I went through stimulus withdrawal: no fresh bagels on the corner, no intellectual frenzy of conversation, no subways and taxis. Now I get clean air and expansive starry skies. I still miss many of the people I knew in New York. Their robust spirits often took hold of my own, like Zaine.

Zaine was the little girl who lived on the top floor of my tenement. The year she was three, Zaine wore a crinoline slip under everything all year long. Her favorite outfit was a ruffled jean skirt, the crinoline peeping from under its hem. Black tights with multi-colored polka dots and pink high top Converse sneakers completed her getup.

But Zaine's ultimate fashion signature was her fairy wings. She wore them on Halloween and from that day forward. In the middle of winter, dressed in crinoline attire and bundled to the hilt, her fairy wings fluttered from the back of her winter coat. For one year, the wings never left her.

In my old neighborhood, folks didn't notice bizarre attire, or at least they pretended not to. People would outdo themselves to create unique looks. In New York, the odd is the norm and normal is odd. Nevertheless, in this neighborhood of eccentric folks, we all noticed Zaine. How could you not spot fairy wings?

Zaine served as the avatar of enlightened imagination. Zaine taught me to appreciate the capacity children have to be what they believe they can be. Zaine was a fairy that year, all year, living in whimsy wherever she went, the winged ideal of a free-spirited, uninhibited child.

Summer's languid days are dwindling. Schedules and order now take over. The back-to-school hubbub has started. Need evidence? Come with me to

Walmart and marvel at aisles of shiny laminate binders and twelve-pack sets of No. 2 pencils. There, I am reminded of Zaine and start my quest for my own fairy wings. So far, no luck. But, I'm undaunted. When I do find them, I'll start a brigade. Any adult is welcome. You just need a desire to ignite that sacred childhood spark. But be forewarned: if you get there before me, just remember, the pink ones with silver glitter are mine.

KAAREN SOLVEIG ANDERSON

PENGUINS

One night not long ago, a little girl was being tucked into bed by her mother. The mom, although tired and cranky, still remembered to go through the ritual of tuck, listen, cuddle, and kiss. She was trying to do it quickly this evening, for dishes, laundry, and other work still stood between her and her own collapse into bed. Thus, the mother was only half-aware when her daughter began speaking.

"My birds come to me in my sleep, Mom."

"What?" asked the mother, startled.

"My birds, you know, the penguins." The child sat up and pointed to a zoo poster over her bed on which appeared a long line of penguins sitting on an ice floe, the bright pink and purple winter sky behind them.

"Your birds come to you in your sleep?" By now the mother was fully awake and listening intently.

"Yes. That one, and that one, and that one, and especially the baby one." She chose three black and white individuals, recognizing something special in their appearance, and concluded with the furry gray immature penguin at the end of the line.

"What do they do, when they come to you in your sleep?" The woman watched her daughter curiously.

"They bring me good gifts." She smiled shyly and lay back down. "They take me outside to show me the sky. And sometimes they fold their wings over my eyes like this to bring me beautiful thoughts." She folded her arms over her face. Her demonstration done, the child turned over. "Good night, Mom."

"I love you. Good night, sweetheart." The mother concluded the ritual with a kiss, stood up, and left the room amazed and delighted.

Months earlier, during a trip to the local zoo, she had given the child a choice of several posters. All but one showed a bright, colorful menagerie of various animals in beautiful environments. The girl had refused the more colorful posters and chose the line-up of penguins. How dull, the mother had thought. How unimaginative, compared to white tigers, alligators, or toucans. She had reluctantly agreed to the girl's choice, concluding that she must not have encouraged her daughter to be daring or adventurous if the girl chose a bunch of black and white penguins over a jungle scene or a florescent coral reef.

Later that evening, the mother took a deep breath as she did the dishes. She realized she was the one who lacked imagination. Focused on her own ideas about color and design, she had missed the beauty and magic in the penguin poster and in her own daughter's mind. The penguins had brought her a "good gift." It was a reminder to be humble in the presence of the mystery of each human heart.

JANE ELLEN MAULDIN

PERCEPTION

I am 27 years old. I was thinking about it the other day. It is very interesting.

I have always been 27 years old. When people said I was 9 years old, and 12 years old, and 19 years old, I knew they were wrong. I was a tall, slim, 27-year-old man with dark brown hair, my own gray sport coat, and imported beer in the refrigerator. I was never a boy or an adolescent. I do not know why people were confused. I knew what I was.

I will always be 27 years old. If people say I am 30 years old, and 45 years old, and 63 years old, I know they are wrong. I am a tall, slim, 27-year-old man with dark brown hair, two gray sport coats, and a bottle of Alka-Seltzer in the cupboard. I will never be middle-aged or a senior citizen. I do not know why people are joking. I know what I am.

I was once shown a picture (said to be of me) of a little boy. He was a skinny little runt with a silly smile and tennis shoes. Who would ever have wanted to be that little boy? Not me! As long as I live, I will be 27 years old, even though parents, teachers, and the police have treated me like a younger person. They did not know my age.

Last week, a man on the television (with my name) looked very old. There was gray on his hair and not on his coat. He was not so slim. Who would ever want to grow up like that? Not me! I am fortunate for being only 27 years old—no matter what happens in the outside world. People do not see everything. What do they know? I know what I will always be.

I learned yesterday that Ginger, my wife, is 19 years old. She has always been 19 years old. She said so herself. I am glad to be a little older. We will never change. How old are you?

DAVID O. RANKIN

SIMPLE PLEASURES

I prefer the modest joys, the understated incarnations, the distilled moments of simple pleasure that are sneaky blessings to everyone:

> the capacity to play and to be renewed by a restful sleep, the whole range of tastes from sweet to bitter and the mysteries in between, the delicate slender fingers of an infant child, the color of sky and sea and the vast complex of hues that melt through the eyes, the sheer wonder of sound shaking the inner soul with tones of depths and heights, the tender remembrance of times that were good and whole, the rustic places that lunged out and lodged in the heart, the persons who shared their secret loves in moments beyond all measuring, the coming of day and the sureness of the return of night, the loyalty of a pet when humans forget to care, the aloneness of solitude that stirs the mind in new directions, the muted meanings that each of us finds in the cycle of life and that hold fast through the fearful rhythms, and all of the subtle and lumbering awarenesses that pulse in us—

for which our hearts sing their joyful "Amen!"

DAVID O. RANKIN

OUR COMMON DESTINY

OUR COMMON DESTINY

First, I must begin with my own creation. I must celebrate the miracle of evolution that resulted in a living entity named David. I must assist in the unfolding of the process by deciding who I am, by fashioning my own identity, by creating myself each day. I must listen to the terrors, the desires, the impulses that clash in the depths of my soul. I must know myself, or I will be made and used by others.

Second, I must learn to affirm my neighbor. I must respect others, not for their function, but for their *being*. I must put others at the center of my attention, to treat them as ends, and to recognize our common destiny. I must never use people to win glory, or to measure the ego, or to escape from responsibility. I must listen to their words, their thoughts, their coded messages.

Finally, I must value action more than intention. I must feel, think, judge, decide, and then risk everything in acts of gratuitous freedom. I must batter the walls of loneliness. I must leap the barriers of communication. I must tear down the fences of anonymity. I must destroy the obstacles to life and liberty. Not in my mind (as a wistful dream), but in my acts (as a daily reality).

DAVID O. RANKIN

THE HOLEY ROBE

Graduation day from seminary was a big event. My mother flew in from another state to cheer me on. Together we remembered the many sacrifices we both had made to get me that far, and we laughed and cried together through the morning. As the time for the ceremony drew near, my mother proudly unpacked my doctoral robe from the factory packing box and volunteered to iron out the many wrinkles. She borrowed an ironing board and a small student travel iron from a seminary housemate, setting them up in the community dining room as I went to prepare myself.

Suddenly I heard a scream of terror and my mother came running down the hall, sobbing, clutching the robe. "I'm so, so sorry, Jane!! I've ruined it! I've ruined it! I couldn't find my reading glasses and I ironed it with the heat too high!" Sure enough, the first doctoral robe ever to be worn by a member of our family had a notable hole, clearly the shape of a travel iron, in the underside of a voluminous sleeve. We hugged and together bemoaned the fate of the robe. There wasn't much to do at the moment. The ceremony would begin in minutes in the church across the street. We wiped our eyes, grabbed our things, and ran.

As I dashed into the church foyer and found my place in a procession just about to begin, my colleagues bent over me in grave concern.

"Where were you?"

"Are you okay?"

I showed them the branded sleeve.

"Oh, that's too bad," said one classmate.

"It will cost a lot to get that sleeve replaced," remarked another, "probably over $100" (an impossible sum for a new seminary graduate).

Then I heard the voice of my friend Patricia, "Why, I think that's dear! Every time you wear your robe, you'll have the memory of your mother with you."

She was right. I have grown to love that sweet hole in my robe. Through it I am connected to my mother and my family. With it I carry all the strength and the pain that I have felt in my family. It reminds me that most of us are "walking wounded," and although the wounds don't always show, they help make us who we are, and help prepare us for the joys and trials of life.

JANE ELLEN MAULDIN

PIECING THE QUILT

My friend Marcy is a tough woman: a lawyer by trade, opinionated, erudite. She is not one you mess with. On occasion she can exhibit a tender side. She can sing you to sleep with a seventies pop medley that stretches her range (vocally) and your own as to what is comforting. She has an uncanny ability to laugh at herself and life. But, sappy? Never. Not her. At least, I didn't think so until I heard the story of her childhood quilt.

Marcy is one in a family of five kids. As a kid, she relied on a yellow and white quilt for security. Given to her at her birth, she carried it around with her wherever she went: grocery shopping, to the movies, to Grandma's . . . she was a regular Linus. One day her mother decided that she was sick of seeing this undoubtedly worn, dirty, scraggly blanket. If my experience at all matches hers, Marcy's mother was mostly sick of looking for it, in those hours of panic and loss, as she ran around the house searching under couches, chairs, in closets, cupboards, hoping to end her daughter's whining. She was determined to wean her daughter of the blanket.

Once a week, for about six months, Marcy's mother would snip off parts of her blanket, making it smaller and smaller. Marcy said if nothing else it got easier to carry, and was serving its purpose, at least from her mother's perspective. At the end of six months, Marcy was left with a palm-size blanket. She continued to use it through her nightly medley to her sisters. She'd still pull the fabric through her forefinger and thumb, in a slow rhythmic fashion. She persisted in sleeping with the remnant of her quilt, a small vestige of comfort and childhood days gone by.

When she told me this story, I was in tears—the image of this child with a now two-inch-by-two-inch blanket had me in fits of laughter. I could just picture her rubbing the piece of fabric against her cheek and inhaling the comforting aroma. I don't think I need to remind you that most children's blankets get odiferous pretty quickly considering they manage to wipe, rub, and spill everything on them. But Marcy says, "I loved that smell." In truth, I was amazed that the cutting of the blanket didn't bother her that much. As long as she had a piece of her quilt left, she was quite content.

Most of us are like my friend Marcy with a two-inch-by-two-inch quilt that says this is who I am. A piece that needs the community spirit of ministering to one another, to make it into a whole piece, a quilt. Some of our pieces are in need of repair, of healing, of patching. They need to be sewn or mended. Others show signs of care already taken with minute, careful, precise stitches. Still others are fixed with Scotch tape or staples. I like to think of church as a gathering place to bring our shredded and worn quilt pieces together—to share. It is in this symbolic action of piecing our lives and stories together into one, in all our diversity of pieces, that makes our quilts whole and healing. Not only for ourselves, but for all of us who will get the benefit of the quilt when we are most broken, most in need of care.

When we come together to piece and sew and mend, we bind ourselves to one another, taking that which makes us most human to share with our pew mates. That is the work of the real quilter, putting the pieces together. Every now and then I get glimpses of the quilt of my church. It is most satisfying when everyone has taken out their needles to explain, revise, and exemplify various mending techniques or sewing skills. Piecing one life to another. Binders, quilters, we.

KAAREN SOLVEIG ANDERSON

HONORING THY FATHER

When I was eight years old, he hit me in the face with a pork chop for talking back to his wife. But he was the gentlest man I have ever known.

When I was nine years old, he encouraged me to learn to defend myself on the streets. But he could always wrestle me to the ground with one arm.

When I was ten years old, I informed him that I was going to run away from home. He offered to buy me a bus ticket and told me to take a winter jacket.

When I was eleven years old, he announced it was time I work for a living. I was employed as a golf ball retriever, but he never recommended a particular career.

When I was fifteen years old, he presented the first and only lecture on sex education. It was only one brief sentence, somewhat muffled, unspeakably graphic, and forever useful.

When I was eighteen years old, he shook my hand and sent me off to college. I was thereafter known as one of those "damn college kids!"

When I was twenty years old, he told me I could have a car, if I bought it with my own money, paid all the bills, and promised not to cruise around.

When I was twenty-one years old, he took me to his favorite tavern and bought me a beer. We talked about baseball and politics but never returned.

When I was twenty-three years old, he wrote me a letter on the presidential election. It was one of the few times he ever asked me a real question—or sought my advice.

A few months later, he died.

He was my father, but I never knew him well.

DAVID O. RANKIN

THE CAT LADY

May Day was a religious institution in my family. My father imparted the tradition of May baskets at a young age, and we never missed the event until I was a sophomore in high school. Each April 30 or so, we would trek down to Guth's Candy on Main Street and carefully select barrel candy for our neighbor's basket. Racing home with our soon-to-be-distributed stash, we discussed hiding spots, and whose house would get the sacred honor of being first. On the first of May, construction paper baskets lined the wagon, overflowing with hard candy, popcorn, and Wisconsin Wood Violets.

Tradition held that baskets were left on someone's front doorknob. You then rang their doorbell and ran away quickly to hide in the bushes at the edge of the lot to wait. Most neighbors followed a predictable pattern. Agitated, they'd stomp out to the porch and look around for the vile youth engaging them in what they thought was an unfriendly game of ding-dong ditch. But eventually they'd spot the benign basket hanging on their doorknob. Smiling now, their eyes scanned the yard for suspects as they gently picked the basket from the handle and retreated inside, as if embarrassed that they had thought the worst.

Conversely, if you knew the tradition, like my neighbor, you wore your running shoes in anticipation. Tradition held that when a May basket was left, the occupant of the house had to run after the child in question and shower them with affection in thanks for their generosity. In my neighbor's case, that meant getting kissed all over your face like an enthusiastic adolescent Lab. You were left with a dewy residue as an emblematic symbol of his thankfulness and virility.

I never outran my neighbor David until I was a freshman in high school. By that time he was in his late fifties, and as I saw it, youth had its advantages (I got tackled hard by his twenty-something son that year—I hadn't managed to outrun the whole family yet).

My sister and I kept one person on our list for last—an elderly woman who wore mismatched clothes and house slippers. At least I thought they were house slippers, but it was hard to tell because she rarely left her house long enough to breathe in fresh air. When she did, she parked her big, foreboding red Cadillac at the bottom of her side stairs only to slide into her house, leaving the neighborhood kids thirty-second glances at best. She lived with her equally reclusive husband, and together they shared a house with twenty or so cats.

Every year my emotions were mixed about going to her house, the dominant emotion being discomfort. My dad, however, gently coaxed us on, encouraging us to not forget the "cat lady." He never insisted, just expressed his opinion that "it might be a good idea, that's all."

And every year, my fear vanished with her reaction. With doorbell rung, she'd walk out her front door, holding the door wide for two or three cats to ramble out for joint inspection. Her hands would fly up in jubilant surprise. Swiping the basket, she too would scan the yard, but then yell out *"Thankkkkkk youuuu!"*—loud enough for the entire neighborhood to hear. Hoisting up one of her cats, she then discussed the contents of the basket with the cat, as if it understood perfectly, leaving us privilege to each little "ooooh" and "aaaah" and "Oh my, isn't this just exquisite!" She would tuck the wood violets behind her ear, only to disappear into her house once again to become the mysterious "cat lady."

I never once walked home without feeling grand somehow. All our efforts were met in that single *"Thankkkkkk youuuu!!"* The "cat lady" was an odd duck in some ways. Up until her, our route included generosity to those who were comfortable, neat, and orderly. Her thank you was an added benefit. But the grand piece of life came from our own need to verify that generosity need not play to a perfect house. Her thank you was a nice added touch, but in truth, it's what the act did to me that made life grand. Her house made the whole event meaningful. Her house changed our sweet little generous act to something larger. All because it wasn't so neatly put together. She changed me, expanded me, challenged me. I think of her now and can only think to yell back, "*Thankkkkkk youuuu!*"

KAAREN SOLVEIG ANDERSON

LIFE JACKETS

My daughter is not learning to swim. At least, not as fast as I would like her to learn. Liz has been taking swimming lessons for the past two summers and all she can do is paddle a few feet across the pool.

My daughter isn't afraid of the water. She splashes and kicks with abandon, regularly pestering any available parent to swim with her in our backyard pool. You see, Liz doesn't *want* to learn to swim. She isn't ready to take her feet off the bottom of the shallow end and trust her body to the strength of her arms and legs.

The problem for me is that I want Liz to be safe and independent in the pool.

The problem for Liz is quite different: she doesn't want to swim, but she does want to follow her big brother and friends into the deep end, to have full range of the entire pool. An inflatable ring or kickboard is bulky and limits her ability to use her arms to play. There have been no easy answers for Liz.

Until now. I stopped at a yard sale a couple of weeks ago and picked up a child's life jacket in good, but used, condition. Liz claimed it for her own immediately. Now when she enters the pool, she tentatively splashes by herself for a few minutes, then pulls on the jacket and joy streams across her face. She feels free and safe with the life jacket on, and I finally have relented to her request to wear it often.

I want Liz to grow, to become independent and self-reliant. She isn't ready yet. For me, that life jacket represents her need to hang on, if only for a few days or weeks—or even a summer—to her childhood.

Many of us have life jackets: people, beliefs, prayers, or habits that support us through the difficult moments of life. They remind us, when we wear them, that in the Great Swimming Pool of Life, we need the buoyancy provided by a larger spirit, a larger purpose, a larger humanity.

Sometimes, when addiction or destruction is the fabric of our life jackets, we really need to remove them. However, when our life jackets are woven of love, they can be true lifesavers.

There was a time in my life when absolute self-reliance appeared the most honest, dependable route to take. Now I trust myself to my husband's love. I trust myself to the trees outside my window, and the air I breathe, and the god-spirit-holiness-interconnectedness of the universe. I trust that I am not alone, even in my most desolate moments.

I continue to encourage Liz to let go and swim. But only she will know the right time. When she does, I believe she will find that an even greater life jacket—the strength of the universe which runs through her veins—will not let her down. Liz will learn to trust and swim. So, I pray, shall we all.

JANE ELLEN MAULDIN

COMBING

In the gospel of Matthew, Jesus is reported to have said, "The very hairs of your head are numbered." Nowadays, when I pull out my comb, I am reminded that the calculation includes a good bit of subtraction in recent years. The consequence of that evolution is that I use my comb more often. This is a development that I had not anticipated. Shouldn't more require greater attention than less? But, indeed, the effort seems far greater now that there is less. Perhaps I should not be surprised that considerable work is required to get the greatest possible effect out of a limited resource.

Applications of this phenomenon occur to me often. We may all soon be learning the new artistry of making less do more for us and others. Less, rather than more, is likely to be a distinguishing characteristic. We may look back upon the present time, with its raucous shouts for "more! more!" to have been the last gasp of the few in a world of limited resources and an expanding population. It is a useful, but demanding, art: doing more with less, and being able to say *enough* rather than *more*. There was little challenge to making hundreds of hairs cover a single half-inch square. A few quick swipes and the job was done. Not so today. For each strand must pull its weight a hundredfold: no shirkers, no extra margin to conceal a hasty, slipshod job. Ah, but how gratifying when it comes out right.

The greatest art reveals no superfluity. The art of the sumi painter is to make each stroke of the brush count. The art of the Japanese flower arranger is to make every element play a role in the loveliness of the whole. Nothing extra, nothing that does not count.

Our material resources may not be the only aspect to benefit from this artistry of economy. Time also may be used in such a way as to make each fragment count for something. As the time remaining diminishes (as it does continuously for each of us), the consciousness of its slipping away adds impetus and urgency to time utilization. I note that the busiest people seem to have the most time. They use it with such care and artistry. Such artistry of economy may be a life-and-death matter, I am reminded as I take up my comb for one more swipe across the increasingly barren landscape of scalp.

GORDON B. McKEEMAN

TRUCK DRIVER

The other day I was driving on an expressway. These days expressway driving seems a frantic enterprise. Near one of the exit ramps, one of the highway denizens, a behemoth "semi" had pulled over onto the berm. The driver had emerged and was gathering some wild plants along the side of the road.

In that moment another stereotype bit the dust. I know what truck drivers are like. They are strong, burly masters of profanity, rootless gypsies who have neither homes nor families. They care not a whit for sunsets, mountain peaks, seashores, or wildflowers. But now I have seen one take the time to stop and look carefully at the splendor by the roadside. I've been by that very spot numerous times. Not once did I take the time or trouble to stop and look at the miracles of leaf and flower. Goodbye, shattered image! I think I shall not miss you at all! You were, it should be said, quite convenient. You allowed me the luxury of not having to think of truck drivers as real people, as varied as the vast diversity of wildflowers.

Stereotypic thinking does not impart solidity or dimensionality to an object. Quite the opposite: It dispenses with the details and eliminates the idiosyncrasies of individuals by making them members of a class of things, all of which have identical characteristics. Well, all truck drivers do have a common characteristic—they do drive trucks. That may exhaust the list of characteristics they share. There's one of them, at least, who notices what is growing beside the road. Quite a feat, actually, at seventy miles an hour.

As the number of people inhabitating our little globe grows, so, I suppose, will the temptation to group people into classes, apply labels to them, and mistake the label for the far more complex reality. Perhaps the image of the truck driver stopping to gather wildflowers by the side of the road can be a reminder of how perilous, how depersonalizing, how diminishing such stereotypes can be. I've had a number of stereotypes pasted on me. As I pause to think about them, I like my own name better than any one of them. I have a hunch that others like their names as well, far better than a label and far, far better than a number. The struggle to maintain a sense of importance for each of us may be long and often difficult. The challenge is quite extraordinary every ordinary day.

GORDON B. MCKEEMAN

MONARCHS AND MYSTERY

I am frequently astonished by monarch butterflies. Delicate beyond belief, they fly thousands of miles each year from all parts of the continent to settle in the forests of South America. To my delight, their migratory route takes them along a bridge near my home.

A few days ago, I was driving on this bridge during their annual display of fragility and strength. As my car whipped by at over sixty miles per hour, the tiny creatures were tossed haphazardly by the winds, yet I knew there was a continual southward purpose to their struggle.

Much as I admired these fragile butterflies, I could not avoid hitting several of them. While orange wings smashed into my windshield, I remembered a chilling science fiction story I had read as a child. A man of the near future travels back in time to the age of the dinosaurs to sightsee in that era. Despite the tour guide's warnings, he leaves the path in his excitement and while in the underbrush steps on and kills one tiny, fragile butterfly. When he returns to his own time, the world is horribly different: people are much crueler and an international fascist government now rules. The death of one butterfly in the distant past has changed all of world history.

As I travel the many miles of the bridge during the annual monarch butterfly migration, I wonder if I am wreaking any changes in the world to come. What effect do my words and deeds—both on the bridge and off—make in the environment and in the human world? Surely they do make a difference. Our kindness affects lives we will never see. Our cruelty casts ripples that may drown strangers.

Whether smashing butterflies or helping a friend, our actions will echo through history. We will not always know the ramifications of our deeds, but they are there. We are surely connected, one to another, and each of us to the greater world of monarchs and mystery.

JANE ELLEN MAULDIN

LEFTOVERS

I sometimes enjoy cooking. I've discovered that one of the greatest of culinary skills is making new creations out of leftovers. It takes imagination. It takes a little skill with spices, herbs, and sauces. The achievement of a satisfying and palatable meal from leftovers can be a model of how one might conduct one's own life in a creative way.

The first thing you need to do is to open the refrigerator door. You'll see an assortment of things: containers, jars, bags, boxes, and things wrapped in foil, waxed paper, or plastic.

Now I invite you to open a different door, the door of your past. What you find there will be leftovers, too. You will probably find your parents' voices, their admonitions, perhaps their praise, maybe their blame, their warnings, some expressions of their love, their anxiety. You may find traces of their uncertainties, problems, and hopes.

You will rediscover some decisions that you have made without thorough understanding of the consequences: about leaving home or not leaving; about when you decided to be married or not to be, or both, and to whom. You will probably remember some of the jobs you took, some of the jobs you wanted but didn't get, and some of the ones you thought about and turned down. You will also find some circumstances, accidents, diseases, and the times you were born into and lived through. You will find your family and some of its ways, its heritage, its customs, the habits that were funny or odd and are somehow deeply ingrained and make other ways seem even odder than your own. You will find people who touched your life in a thousand unaccounted and unexpected ways, who were there at special moments and changed you or made you a gift: the gift of a smooth stone, a happy day, or an unforgettable experience. And there will be all the ruins, sorrows, guilts, regrets, along with the fears and the hopes, dreams and doubts, forgivings and forbiddings. Don't we have crowded refrigerators! Everyone of us, such a collection of leftovers.

In making a life, we're all cooking with leftovers from childhood, even infancy. The longer we're at it, the more leftovers there are. Of course, people are always looking for the "big answer" and there is one big answer to cooking with leftovers. You open the door, and you are faced with the problem, What can I make of it? I take that to be the secret ingredient for dealing with leftovers. A scriptural version is "the substance of things hoped for, the evidence of things not seen." You might consider attaching it to the refrigerator door—either the internal one or the external one—since it's a description that fits both. What is that secret ingredient? It is, of course, faith. "Faith is the substance of things hoped for, the evidence of things not seen."

Welcome to the world where we all cook using leftovers—some of us with imagination, some with creativity, some merely resenting the task, some thinking there is no possibility in it. Add the secret ingredient. Something will come of it that will be at least edible, probably even palatable.

GORDON B. McKEEMAN

BEING HUMAN

To be human is to be in touch with the larger rhythms and harmonies of the universe;

To be human is to be aware of the beauty of a creation that continually unfolds;

To be human is to be the servants of the earth upon which our existence depends;

To be human is to embrace the present moment as a sacred, joyful occasion;

To be human is to nurture bridges of intimacy that are global and inclusive;

To be human is to be in a state of process: to live, to love, and to never die.

DAVID O. RANKIN

WE ARE PART OF THE CIRCLE

WE ARE PART OF THE CIRCLE

My wakeful nights are fewer now that my children are growing older. A recent event reminded me of what I am missing. After a tremendously exciting weekend in another state at a family celebration, my young son and I found that our sleep schedules were no longer in sync.

On the way home, Ben slept in the plane and the car and then was awake in his room from 10:00 p.m. until 3:00 a.m. Meanwhile, I was completely, utterly, absolutely exhausted. My husband joined me in physical oblivion because he had just spent the weekend at home, getting up often throughout the nights with a baby daughter who missed her mother. An old back injury was also troubling Harry and he lay drugged, with ice on his back, in great pain.

It was a thousand and one nights that night. Each time I fell asleep, Ben called for me. He was disturbed, afraid, and insecure after his intense weekend of travelling and meeting new people. I grew grumpier and grumpier, padding through a sleeping household to reassure and calm a wakeful child. I felt alone and adrift, aware that I alone could help the child who called out to me, yet desperately needy myself.

I spent the next day with my eyes open yet with brain cells barely functioning. Although exhausted,

I slowly recalled a truth that has helped me to carry on: As I trudged alone through the night hallways, I staggered to a call as old as humankind. That night and every night, mothers and fathers around the world awaken to reassure restless children. That night and every night, grown children arise to calm fitful, aging parents. Those night hours are long and lonely. Our burdens and tired bones are ours alone to bear. There are, however, other people out there who are waking even as we are. There are other people who bear similar burdens—whether it is simply to reassure a child for one night, or to help a dying loved one be at peace, week after week, until the end.

We who rise do so because we choose to do it. It is an intense, physical demand; it is also an honor as ancient as human love. We are part of the circle of families and friends who nurture Life, from its earthly beginning until its earthly conclusion.

JANE ELLEN MAULDIN

ANYONE'S MINISTRY

Ministry is

a quality of relationship between and among
human beings

that beckons forth hidden possibilities;

inviting people into deeper, more constant
more reverent relationship with the world
and with one another;

carrying forward a long heritage of hope and
liberation that has dignified and informed
the human venture over many centuries;

being present with, to, and for others
in their terrors and torments
in their grief, misery, and pain;

knowing that those feelings
are our feelings, too;

celebrating the triumphs of the human spirit,
the miracles of birth and life,
the wonders of devotion and sacrifice;

witnessing to life-enhancing values;
speaking truth to power;

standing for human dignity and equity,
for compassion and aspiration;

believing in life in the presence of death;
struggling for human responsibility
against principalities and structures
that ignore humaneness and become
instruments of death.

It is all these and much, much more than all of
them, present in
    the wordless,
    the unspoken,
    the ineffable.

It is speaking and living the highest we know
and living with the knowledge that it is
    never as deep, or as wide
    or as high as we wish.

Whenever there is a meeting
that summons us to our better selves, wherever
    our lostness is found,
    our fragments are united,
    or our wounds begin healing,
    our spines stiffen and
    our muscles grow strong for the task,

there is ministry.

GORDON B. MCKEEMAN

GERDA'S RASPBERRY

In August, I trekked to Boston for a day of books—
my annual trip to browse, review, and buy inspira-
tional and theological texts. After two hours, I
started off for the train station. I wasn't in my typical

hurry, so I stopped at the Holocaust Memorial, something I had previously walked quickly past. Names of hundreds of thousands of survivors towered over me, neatly written on giant plexiglass monuments. At eye level, sayings and quotes by survivors are etched into the structures. I got stuck in front of one. For five minutes, my feet cemented themselves to the pavement below me. I watched the construction workers eat their sandwiches from sturdy metal lunch boxes, listening to them discuss the intricacies of Sunday's football game. A busload of kids walked around me, engrossed in the woes of seventh-grade life.

But the world stopped for a while as I, feet still stuck, read and re-read the quote. Tears trickled out. Are there words to describe that feeling of horror that only a guttural, animalistic voice can reveal? An exhaling of breath that fights hard to return? Any memorial can do that to you, a witness and testament to injustice, pain, oppression.

I jotted down the quote on a piece of paper and brought it home. This tiny piece of paper received its own folder. I'd open it up, read the quote, and re-file, only to pick it up a few days later. It was magnetic. The words were by Gerda Weisman Klien: "Ilse, a childhood friend of mine, once found a raspberry in the camp and carried it in her pocket all day to present to me that night on a leaf. Imagine a world in which your entire possession is one raspberry and you give it to a friend."

I tried to imagine. I tried to put myself in Gerda's place, in Ilse's place. I couldn't. I would sit on the back steps of my house, eyes closed, trying to imagine the misery, the wonder of a such a gift, the selflessness of the act. I couldn't get there. Until one day with a raspberry pint resting in my lap, I'd lift one up and think of gifts given. Selfless giving by others: my mother's words of comfort the day I came home from school humiliated that I had been the first to misspell a word in the spelling bee; my sister's half smile and strong hands clenching mine as she whispered comforting words to me past drones of machines, pumps, and tubes during my ICU internment hell; my lover's words to me that to him I am Grace, I am Home. With each thought, I ate a raspberry. Something previously unimaginable now took shape, my vessel of life was full, filled with gifts. I felt Gerda's words and life in a way I couldn't comprehend before, by getting to the gifts that were given to me, all residing within, like well-eaten raspberries.

KAAREN SOLVEIG ANDERSON

AFTER THE HURRICANE

A few days after Hurricane Andrew devastated southern Florida and parts of Louisiana, I heard someone neatly wrapping up the events in Bad Theology. I was listening to my favorite public radio program when a report described a worship service in a Florida church that had been mildly damaged in the hurricane. Volunteers had mended the few holes in the roof with donated plywood, and worship services continued. The minister, however, found deep significance in the lack of major harm done to the building.

"I have driven by Lakeside Baptist Church. It is *gone*!" he roared. "I have driven by Main Street Baptist Church. It is *gone*! I have even driven down to Believers' Baptist Church. It is *gone*! God has spared us!" he concluded. "God has spared *us*!"

How easy it is for some people to examine the conditions of their lives and to conclude that they are better loved by the powers of the universe than a Somalian woman with three children starving in the desert. How easy it is for some people living in comfortable conditions to believe that they deserve all they have and that a man born and raised in inner city slums deserves his lot in life, too.

It would be easy and comfortable to believe these things, but I do not. I am convinced that we are all interconnected. We are all responsible for one another.

It is hard to choose my words judiciously after hearing such an adamant declaration of Bad Theology. Yet after the sad and sarcastic responses finished playing through my head, one certainty remains: We who believe otherwise must not keep quiet. To keep our message to ourselves allows such Bad Theology to become the Theology of America.

If a radio reporter ever came to my home, I would say that God is the creative force that has cast each of us into this world. God is the love in and between people. God does not willfully direct hurricanes onto the beaches of the unjust. God is the moral conscience that demands we walk these beaches hand-in-hand, building together where hurricanes have destroyed.

JANE ELLEN MAULDIN

MS. PERFECT

Round, brown, doe-like eyes rested near the edge of her glasses. Best described as stout, there was nothing unhurried about her. The skin under her arms swung in pendulum force when she moved due to years of weight fluctuation. My grandmother. Far from a slave to fashion, she nonetheless cared about her appearance, wearing a full-corseted girdle daily. She wasn't ugly or beautiful, yet she sported a quick, one-sided mischievous grin that always kept you guessing as to her womanly guises. She was a klutz of enormous proportions, the trait I inherited. A woman who looked like a grandmother at thirty. It may not have helped that she drove a 1964 Plymouth Valiant with pushbutton transmission, the kind of car that no matter what your age screamed geriatric mobile.

My grandmother was a misfit of sorts. When I was a child, she was my icon of paradox. On one hand she was the mother of comfort. Her house always smelled of overcooked vegetables and well-used wool. When feeling out of sorts, she would promptly offer you her favorite food: Cheese Whiz on toast. On the other hand, nobody could embarrass me as a kid, making me uncomfortable like she could. She would be deep in conversation with someone while concurrently and unabashedly scratching her large bosom, oblivious to the obvious misstep in propriety.

She was queen of malaprop, which at times proved humorous and at others embarrassing. Once she was telling some friends of the family about my cousin's recent abode in Missouri, where she was attending college. "Well, Liv has found such a nice condom to live in, it's beautiful." It took everything in all of us gathered in her living room to bite any part of our mouth in an effort to control our laughter. The image of a house-sized latex condom serving as a condo had us in fits.

This odd woman could weave beauty into lives like none other. An avid, voracious quilter, she was a binder of pieces and parts. She took beauty seriously, and expected the rest of us to do so too. She was the most patient, attentive counselor. When burdened with life's questions and perplexities, her living room was always open, her ear always attuned, her answers measured. She could also give you a biting retort if she believed you to be slothy, unethical, or lazy in behavior.

My grandmother died ten years ago now. I miss her oddness, her quirky character. The older I get, the more I realize she had a lot to teach me—not in family history, or in how to be a quilter, or how to make carnage of fresh vegetables. No, the older I get, the more I think she was perfect. She wasn't a model with flawless features. She wasn't a Nobel Laureate, distinguished, astute, or brilliant. She wasn't even the nicest, kindest, gentlest person I knew. She was perfect because she knew how to be her—Sylvia Anderson. She knew how to be human, not a façade of one. There was no pretense about her, you got what you saw. She fit into her skin, and her skin fit her.

My own skin doesn't always fit so well. I get hung up on vanity, or trying to be hip or cool, or allowing conventional etiquette to rule my behavior or actions. I get in my own way of being me. My skin would fit better if I just remembered more often that wonderful woman I once knew and thought of her greatest gifts of being: contradiction, fallibility, and humor. The makings of a perfect gal.

KAAREN SOLVEIG ANDERSON

MOSQUITO

Sleep's blanket of respite eludes me. Mosquito bites line the arch of my left foot. The bed sheet scrapes my skin with remnant beach sand. The shade beats unevenly against the window sill. I can't sleep. I'm agitated. It doesn't help that the king of irritation buzzes slowly, persistently around my head. I put the covers over my head in an attempt to escape. But then, I can't breathe. I throw them off and come up for air. The impatient whine of the mosquito returns, torturing me, bumping into my temple, and retreating as I swat in vain into the surrounding darkness.

When I was a kid and still believed in God, I used to think mosquitoes were God's agitators. His way of making self-reflection a necessity, a chore.

I was always glad this agitation came in the darkness of the night, so no one else was privy to my tortured confessions. Mosquitoes could get me so uncomfortably awake that I became my own agitator. Agitating thoughts would swell in my head, rushing and reeling around me. Times in my life I wasn't so proud of me. Times I'd rather forget instead of remember. Times when I took advantage of a friend or misled a neighbor. Times I outright lied to cover my own failings, or spoke harshly when words of love were needed. I hated mosquitoes, they made me become my own tormentor. My own filter of conscience and good will. I wanted nothing more than to smash the little bugger buzzing around my head, as well as what was conjured up in my head.

I don't think mosquitoes are God's agitators anymore. I like to think of them as evolutionary justice. Imagine if you will, a mosquito during the dinosaur age. Bumping into those mammoth creatures, trying desperately to agitate, to irritate, to conjure self-reflection. Yet they were met with thick, impervious skin and brains so puny that consciousness-raising was never an option. Now, mosquitoes are in their element. They've come into their own. They feast on soft, gullible, permeable human skin. Skin that not only is sensitive, but captive to a body that holds a conscience, that can appreciate the agitation of the mosquito. A conscience that needs small

irritating reminders that we can do better, reach
for more, envision ourselves grander, kinder, more
. . . well, likable.

Sleep is starting to sweep over me. The mosquito
has had its fill. I close my eyes, and for the first time
ever . . . have dinosaur envy.

KAAREN SOLVEIG ANDERSON

IN-LAWS

For Anne and Richard Lowenburg

They are an older couple. Not so old in years, yet life
has etched its changes on their bodies and circumstances. They have raised and continue to help their
now-grown children. They have been loyal and
loving to their friends. They have cared for aging
parents, giving fully without hesitation or regret.

But now he is ailing. I see them as often as I can,
and each time I leave, I am amazed at my own youth
and how much I have to learn.

Sometimes I try to visit them with my own agenda:
"See here, you should do this, or call that agency, or
read this article." I speak authoritatively with all the
wisdom that four decades of life have bestowed on
me. They listen kindly. They nod, smile, and love me
despite my arrogance. Then I depart and they keep

on caring for one another in the deep and powerful ways they have for some forty years.

I am humbled before such love. I go home tired to my fussy children and stressed husband and immediately hear words come out of my mouth that have no place in a home of love.

So I take a breath and wonder silently how I might develop the patience and forgiveness that are the corollaries of real love. When will I ever learn?

I watch the man and woman greet each day with gentleness and quiet optimism, despite the looming night. They are my teachers, more surely than any who ever taught me my ABCs.

JANE ELLEN MAULDIN

THE KINDNESS OF LO MEIN

My friend Marcy and her boyfriend Brian recently ate dinner at a local Chinese restaurant. As they enjoyed a plate of lo mein, engrossed in conversation, a hand reached down and ushered away their platter of noodles. A voice quick and agitated mumbled "Sorry!" and a thin, poorly dressed woman left the restaurant with their plate of lo mein.

In astonishment, they watched her walk down the street, holding the plate with the flat of her hand as she stuffed noodles into her mouth, slapping sharply against her face. The owner realized what had happened and darted out the front door, chasing after the noodle thief. He stood firmly in front of her, blocking her way and grabbing a side of the plate. A struggle ensued, noodles slid uneasily from one side to the other, slopping over the edge. He surged forward and pulled with a heroic strong-arm attempt to retrieve his plate. The woman's fingers slid from the plate. Noodles flew, then flopped pathetically on the sidewalk.

Left empty-handed, with soggy, contaminated noodles at her feet, the woman stood with arms hung dejectedly at her side. The owner walked victoriously back to the restaurant with the soiled plate in hand. My friends were given a new heaping plate of lo mein, although they had already consumed half of the stolen plate. A stream of apology in Chinese came from the proprietor. Unable to eat anymore, they asked to have the noodles wrapped up and set off to see their movie.

A block later, they happened upon the lo mein thief. The woman was hypercharged. She simultaneously cried, convulsed, and shouted at a man, who rapidly retreated from her side. My friend, unsure about what to do, listened to her boyfriend's plea to just walk away. But she didn't. Instead, she walked over to the thief and said, "Ah, we haven't formally met, but about ten minutes ago, you were interested in our noodles. They gave us some new ones, are you still hungry?" The woman nodded and extended her bony arms. She took the styrofoam container in her hands, bowed ever so slightly, and murmured, "Thank you, you're very kind."

What makes us walk away from discomfort? Or stay? You could say a lot about my friend's story—a lot about generosity, kindness, attention, and thievery. I'm more interested in what motivates us to confront that which makes us uncomfortable and makes us look at the guts and grit of decisions, the choices to not address things that are uncomfortable, uneasy, unbalanced, unnatural, unbelievable. When our foundations start to shake, we can feel the tremors move up our legs and into our torsos. And we want more than anything to make it stop. Any how. Any way.

My friend Marcy could feel herself shake. I know because she told me so. But she chose not to walk away, she dealt with uncomfortableness. She held firm in the muck. Sometimes, that's all we need or can do to get to the other side—the side where generosity, comfort, and kindness reside, the side where foundations are firm and stable. Where one's shaking walks back to the other side.

KAAREN SOLVEIG ANDERSON

TIE TACK

There are many relics in our home—objects to which important memories are attached. You probably have some, too. Each recalls some journey, event, or person that is a part of your life's experience. They're precious on that account—religious objects that summon up powerful recollections. One of my favorites is my tie tack. It's an opal, full of fiery iridescence.

The tie tack was an unexpected gift. Its former owner, the donor, came out of the church's worship one Sunday. As I greeted him, I noticed his tie tack and I said to him, "What a beautiful opal!" On the spot he took it off and gave it to me. I was both delighted and chagrined. I took off my tie tack, a UUSC flaming chalice, and gave it to him. It was far from an equal exchange. More important, what he did in that fleeting moment was very typical of him. He was a person of whom it could be said without exaggeration, "He'd give you the shirt off his back." He lived quite an ordinary life. He was a salesman of advertising novelties, so he spent much time in his car traveling from client to client. He spent a significant portion of his driving time thinking of ways to improve the community. He could be counted on to suggest some modest and simple change that would make a positive and real difference in people's lives. Some of his ideas were real winners, saving much public money and touching many lives with joy and opportunity. My life was one of those.

One of my joys associated with wearing a necktie is to put on my tie tack. I have quite a few of them, but my opal is always my choice. It's a ritual. I put it on and remember the man who gave it to me, and I resolve to find in this day some opportunity to continue what was his real life's work: doing something simple, modest, and useful to improve the life of the community.

Over the many years I have worn my tie tack, many people have admired it. To many of them I have told the story of my acquisition of it and of what it means to me. With each telling I have confessed that I ought to give it away, since that's how I obtained it—by admiring it. Some day I know I will give it away, together with its story. Meanwhile I say that I'm keeping a list of its admirers and offering to add the name of another possible recipient. Meanwhile, I keep wearing it and keep reminding myself of its meaning in my life.

Reflecting on one's relics now and then is a useful spiritual discipline—remembering the events, the persons, the occasions when ordinary things were somehow transformed into religious objects. All around us are the reminders of the days of our lives, the people whose touch was a blessing, a balm, an invitation, a beckoning to be a better person— deeper, more secure, more daring, more generous, more caring. My tie tack does more—much, much more—than hold my tie. On some ordinary day like today, I invite you to consider your relics.

GORDON B. McKEEMAN

ONE'S HANDS

A couple of weeks ago I was perusing football journals and books. I came across a photograph of a lineman. He was watching the field intently, his body hunched against a heavy sleet, his hands free to the elements. I turned the page of the book and there was a close-up of his hands, bent and mangled, covered with scabs, bruises, and scrapes. I was fascinated by his hands. Hands he would inevitably have to soothe. Hands that held violence and pain but also gentleness.

I put the book down and gazed at my own hands and thought about them: what they touch and experience and create. I already have my grandmother's hands with index fingers twisting slightly inward. I have bulbous veins winding under the skin that speak to my life: typing, playing the piano, soothing hurts, applying bandages, caressing, and daily work.

I like to look at farmers' hands or fishermen's hands. Laboring hands. Hands that speak to the life of the person. I don't want smooth hands; I want mine to speak to my person, to my life's work, to a sum of my parts. A place I can look and see generations before and after me, of work started or incomplete.

I have a colleague who is often present with people when they die. Once I asked her what she did. Did she have some ritual for the passing of a life? She said she helps wash the body. She washes the face as a symbol of what that person has seen, the hands as a symbol of what that person has done, and the feet as a symbol of where that person has been.

I love that symbolism. Unlike the lineman who can look at his hands and see what he does, most of us can forget what it is we do, and who we are connected to. But it's all there, in our hands. Those we touch or greet in welcome and friendship, of creation made possible through writing or painting or playing, of conversations retold, of tears shed in cradled hands.

The Shakers have a saying, "Hands to work, and Hearts to God." They believe that your life's calling —your work—should be no less than an act of joy. An act of work is an act of worship.

I stare at my hands and whisper, Amen.

KAAREN SOLVEIG ANDERSON

A DROP IN THE BUCKET

What it says about inadequacy, futility, insignificance!
   A drop in the bucket. What's the sense? What's
      the use?
We're no longer in the center of things.
   Copernicus removed the earth from the center
      of the solar system. Darwin removed humans
      from the center of the earth. Astronomy has
      removed the solar system from the center of
      the universe.
Well, who are we, then, and where are we?
   Physiologists call us "weak, watery solutions,
      more or less jellified."
   Mark Twain said, "Man is the only animal
      that blushes—or needs to."
Just suppose that we are the merest drops in a bucket.
   There are unspoken assumptions here.
   We assume that a full bucket is what we're aiming at
      and that until the bucket is full, nothing has
      been accomplished.
   There is never a shortage of buckets. The empty
      bucket litany is long and tedious: racism,
      sexism, ableism, authoritarianism, oppression,
      injustice, violence, environmental degradation,
      overpopulation.
   You feel like a drop in the bucket? Who asked
      you to *fill* the bucket—especially all alone?

Remember how many there are who share your concern. We may feel daunted, but we are not one drop. A sense of isolation is the parent of the drop-in-the-bucket feeling.

Sometimes one can decide the size of the bucket. Don't think you can do a large bucket? Try a smaller size. Even imparting a bit of hope— a pat on the back, a financial contribution, a few hours of volunteer service—every drop helps!

It might even be wise to remember

why you need to help fill *this* bucket, possibly to quench the thirst of someone hard at work on a larger one

that buckets of whatever size are filled a drop at a time. If you don't help, it will take even longer.

that your drop may be one of the last ones needed. (Why is it that our image is of the first drop in the bucket?)

where we'd be if everybody gave up putting drops in the bucket—probably much worse off.

Persistence depends on patience, on keeping at it when there is little to reassure us. It would be too bad to give up, to sit back, bemoan the sorry state of the world and wonder why somebody, anybody, everybody (but not me, thank you) doesn't do something about "it."

After all, the Grand Canyon was fashioned by
    drops of water,
        as ordinary as they seem.

GORDON B. McKEEMAN

A TIME TO BE SILENT

A TIME TO BE SILENT

There must be a time when we cease speaking
    to be fully present with ourselves.

There must be a time when we exclude clamor
    by listening to nothing whatsoever.

There must be a time when we forgo our plans
    as if we had no plans at all.

There must be a time when we abandon conceits
    and tap into a deeper wisdom.

There must be a time when we stop striving
    and find the peace within.

Amen!

DAVID O. RANKIN

PRAYER OF CAREGIVING

May the burden of caring
not feel so heavy
as I remember all who have
gone before me
and all who will come after me.
May I know myself to be part of a great dance
that circles and comes round again.

I give thanks for the privilege of caring.
I am home. I am home.

JANE ELLEN MAULDIN

DOUBT

An honest "No" is a glorious statement.

Doubt is the expression of faith in the intelligence and imagination of humanity.

Doubt is the expression of humility about the capacity for errors and mistakes.

Doubt is the expression of wisdom when popular and rewarding truths are wrong.

Doubt is the expression of confidence that knowledge can always be improved.

Doubt is the expression of courage in confronting the dangerous and destructive.

Doubt is the expression of hope that a better world is waiting for the future.

Doubt is the expression of harmony with the unceasingly changing universe.

Doubt is the expression of concern for the proper

integration of thought and experience.

It is not evil, but good, an intrinsic element of faith.

DAVID O. RANKIN

INVISIBLE

"Seeing is believing." I suppose so, but that's not
    all there is to it.
There's so much reality that is unseen, invisible.
    My living room is awash in things that arrive
        by routes invisible.
    The television set offers pictures of events
        transpiring half a world away—almost
        instantaneously—through the air and the
        space above it, often reflected (so I'm
        told) by satellite, also mostly invisible
            a flood, a famine, a volcanic eruption
            a coronation, a funeral, an inauguration
            a birth, a battle, a peace conference
            a festival—in full color.
    I don't see it in the air; I do, however,
        believe it, sight unseen.
Oh, but I must take my pills!
    That event launches another unseen process.
    How my body knows where to send all those tiny

particles (so insignificant, save for the
expense) to nourish, stimulate, hold in
check, destroy, inhibit, heal, supplement
is one vast, invisible process that eludes
seeing, even seeing by microscopes.

Not seeing, I do believe.

I drive my car and its radio plucks music, traffic
advisories, weather reports, the latest news
out of the ether on command. There's not just
one message lurking invisibly all about me, but
a whole catalog of choices to be selected by
the twist of a dial or the press of a button.

I don't understand, nor do I see them, but
I do believe.

Human beings, too, send messages that arise from
invisible wellsprings.

I wonder whence cometh the tenacity, the courage,
the tenderness, the aspirations that are the
invisible sources of perseverance, quiet
bravery in the face of pain, love for those
who are sometimes hard to love, hope that
prevails over dark despair.

Whence they come, I cannot see.

But I do believe.

Some wise person once defined religion as an
invisible means of support. Fortunately, there is
great power arising from invisible sources.

May it be your good fortune on this quite ordinary day

to be able to believe in some invisible things that have extraordinary consequences.

GORDON B. McKEEMAN

YES, MAYBE

After a worship service, I was greeting people in the reception line.

"Congratulations," she said. " You read his poetry very well."
"Thank you," I replied.
"Of course, he was not always a happy man," she continued. "His life was a struggle. Hope was hard won. Even in the end, if he affirmed anything at all, it was a yes, maybe."
"You seem to know a lot about him," I said.
"Not everything," she replied. "But I am his daughter."

It was 1974, the one hundredth anniversary of his birth. We were talking about Robert Frost.

If you are a "yes" type of person, you may not understand Robert Frost. He does not speak well to the once-born, to the buoyant and optimistic, to those who are blessed with a happy hope and a cheerful faith.

If you are a "no" type of person, you may not understand Robert Frost. He does not speak well to the life-denying, to the cynical or nihilistic, to those who lack a candle of hope and a spark of faith.

But if you are on the edge, a "yes, maybe" type of person—wrestling with the inner demons, searching to find the meaning of life, clinging with your fingernails to a dim hope and a fragile faith—then you will understand Robert Frost. He is your Advent poet.

DAVID O. RANKIN

YOUR VERY PRESENCE

A number of years ago, my brother lay dying in the hospital. He spent days in the intensive care unit while members of my family, including my mother, sat for many long hours on chairs in the hallway outside his room. Among the visitors who came to share the vigil was a member of our church.

"How are you doing?" the friend asked.

My mother was too exhausted to tell anything but the truth. "I'm tired," she said. "I'm very, very tired. I'm too tired to even pray any more."

"But don't you see," her friend replied, "your very presence here is a prayer."

There are times when all words fail us, all forms seem hollow, and no one out there or inside seems to be listening. At those times, our presence, just our presence, is prayer. Our bodies, our actions, become our prayer, our connection to God, whatever God may be.

JANE ELLEN MAULDIN

REV. BURKUM'S BIBLE

It's the season of Yom Kippur. A time during the Jewish calendar year to say you're "sorry" to not only those you've wronged, but the divine. A time of forgiveness, with the prospect of starting anew. And it's now that I remember.

When I was ten years old, we visited friends of the family. The father of the house was a very large, formidable Lutheran minister. He gave me a little Bible to look at. It was tiny, smaller than my palm, yet it was the Bible in its entirety. I could look at it, but I couldn't have it. Well, I took it. Okay, I stole it. I put it in my pocket and stole it. Later, I'd take it out to admire it, and honor would grab me and shake me. As if it were on fire, I would thrust it back in my desk drawer. I was a thief, of the Bible no less. Finally, I forgot my crime and the object of my shame.

When I was about fifteen and had outgrown the desk, I went through the drawers and found the minuscule Bible. I should have returned it then. I didn't. In fact, I decided not to deal with my emotions about the thing and threw it away. Sacrilege, I know, but it lay in the wastebasket on top of Kleenex and pencil shavings, mocking me. I pushed it to the bottom. Ugh.

Recently, I saw this minister at my sister's wedding. We had a great conversation. In the last couple of years, much grief has passed through his life. He spoke eloquently of my call and how proud of me he was. I couldn't tell him that, truth be told, I was a part-time Bible thief.

I often wonder why I felt so powerless that I acted out by stealing a Bible. I never enjoyed the act or the thing, and in the long run I just felt more powerless. I couldn't even tell him what I had done. I compounded the crime of my childhood with my silence. We adults don't like to feel powerless, or out of control, or wrong.

But, truth be told, I'm wrong a lot. Again: I'm wrong a lot. It is at this time of year, at Yom Kippur, that I'm forced to stand firm and look truth in the eyes and admit to my errors. Yom Kippur helps me look at my deepest darkest yuck and say, well, I'm wrong again, and then to ask for forgiveness, divine and human. It's an agitating holiday, not one that brings comfort and joy, or the promise of rebirth. No, Yom Kippur, I think, offers something deeper: the chance to be honest with ourselves, to touch the tip of our pain, to confront our insecurities, wantonness, abrasiveness, and powerlessness. It's a chance to become truly powerful. To face truth and ask for forgiveness for our imperfect humanity. We tend to mess up a lot. When we can admit that, we move forward and become more fully ourselves.

It's the season of Yom Kippur. I have a wrongdoing list to attend to. Forgiveness to ask for. I just wish the first name didn't start with a Rev.

KAAREN SOLVEIG ANDERSON

RELUCTANT GOODBYES

I hate goodbyes. I hate everything about them. It bothers me that "goodbye" isn't really what I think we most often want to say.

When those I love leave me, or I leave them, goodbye isn't what I want to say. I want to tell them that their warm hand on my cheek, which caught my desperate tears, made me feel whole once again. I want to tell them that without their quick giggle and tender words, my life can feel lonely. But no—instead I tell them, "I love you," give them a hug, and say goodbye. And they leave and I leave. I feel hollow, discontented, and sometimes lost. I didn't want to say goodbye.

When those I am in conflict with leave or I leave them, goodbye isn't what I want to say. I want to talk about pieces of me that are torn, scratched, and fragmented because of our interchanges. I want to tell them that, just maybe, I've learned something new: in how to be, in how to live, in how to grow. I wonder why it got so complicated and sticky. But no—instead we say with fortitude, "Goodbye." I may shake their hand, glad that I won't have to see them again. But there is so much unsaid, and goodbye doesn't skim the root of my feelings. I didn't want to say goodbye.

When time whispers to me, "Move on, here's the next step, say goodbye," I watch as my son walks into his first day of kindergarten, confident, filled with anticipation. These are my people, my life, he is thinking.

"Bye, mom," he yells to me and signs *love*. I sign back.

"Bye," I whisper. But goodbye isn't what I want to say. I want to tell him that he is remarkable, brave, that I need more time to adjust to his boyhood, his self-assurance, his friends. I need more time to let go of one more tiny sliver of him. But no—instead I say goodbye. I feel jolted, awakened to time moving forward without me. I didn't want to say goodbye.

When someone I love dies, goodbye isn't what I want to say. I want to tell them the truth about us. I want to set it straight. Get to what was real. That their words could hurt, that I wasn't as strong as they'd hoped, that I still struggle to forgive them. At the same time, I want to tell them that their love made life easier, freer, more accessible. That I'm grateful for their presence. I want to tell them that I forgive them for being human, hoping they did the same for me. But no—instead we say "goodbye" at a memorial service. And I feel captured in a storm of emotions that violently swirl me around. I didn't want to say goodbye.

When life turns to me someday and says, "Say goodbye," goodbye isn't what I want to say. I'll say, "I've said 'Goodbye' my whole life, let me say it right, now. Just let me say it right." But life's hands will close around me, ushering me to something new. It will be the only time where "goodbye" was what I needed to say.

KAAREN SOLVEIG ANDERSON

DEATH ITSELF

My ministry to the dying, though filled with tears, has been a trial worth enduring.

I have learned that a single human life is the most precious entity in all of God's creation, not to be bartered for a genie's wish or a king's fortune.

I have learned that our abundant existence on earth is too much filled with petty thoughts, trivial concerns, and a meanness toward our fellow creatures.

I have learned that it is good to live with a knowledge of our finitude, as if each moment is our last, so that what we do is a new kind of doing.

I have learned that the fear of death, which arises from our personal fantasies and cultural anxieties, is more to be dreaded than death itself.

And I have also learned that the human being is a marvelous construction, with the faith and courage to confront any power in the universe—even the reaper, whose name is Death.

DAVID O. RANKIN

HOW WILL WE BE REMEMBERED?

Unexpectedly, suddenly, there was someone out of the past—a person remembered, but not fully—a timbre of voice, a familiar glint of eye or shape of face or a distinctive mannerism. And then a name recalled, a summons sent down to the dim recesses of memory to call up the recollections of times past, events long faded into mists of years now gone, but not really gone. Rather years that have been put away to await the summons—to be called back to life.

Lurking there in the shadows are all of our pasts—all the ecstasies, the hurts and harms, the shames and prides, the successes and failures, the ghosts, the familiar figures that haunt our days and nights—summoned forth by sounds unheard to visit us with secret pain or solace.

It does seem strange that we who have such experiences so commonly think that immortality is only a fantasy, a figment of fond hopes that death shall pass us by. Nay, we shall live, the familiar spirits in lives beyond our own.

But since we cannot avoid death, it may be wise for us to consider what messages shall be elicited from our spirits. Will we be ogres from whom others shrink in fear or anguish? Or something more fondly remembered, sustaining with soft messages of love and joy, of courage and confidence, of acceptance and encouragement?

To think thus of ourselves and others recalls a statement attributed to Jesus: "Lo I am with you always." For our memories of the past are not easily brushed aside; nor are they quickly erased. One of the problems with which we wrestle is how to hear the old ghosts without allowing them to rule our future, as they have reigned in our past. While it is impossible to change the past, when the ghosts were

real and regnant, it is not required that we surrender the future to their sway. Let them have their day,
but yield not tomorrow. It belongs to the living.

Are not we all haunted houses, inhabited by
spirits, by loved ones and unloved ones as well? How
spooky, thinking of ourselves as ghostly shades called
up when our name echoes down the halls of another's
unconscious. If you're bound to be a haunting figure
to another, why not a friendly ghost?

GORDON B. MCKEEMAN

THE HEART'S GEOGRAPHY

The relationship between religion and health is
an ancient one, going far back in human history
to shamans, medicine wheels, incantations, and
exorcisms. More recently, Mary Baker Eddy's
Christian Science has attracted many adherents.
Most Unitarian Universalists are more likely to
consult a medical doctor than a minister about
bodily ailments, although other forms of therapy
have numerous devotees.

The relationship between physical health and the
spiritual realm, however, has not disappeared. We are
discovering that illness is more complex than we had
assumed. Among the complexities is the insight that

curing and healing, while related, are not the same. Curing has to do with the elimination of disease. It is the primary province of medicine and surgery. Healing has to do with a more inclusive view of the human being; it is related to the whole of life, not merely to the health (or the lack thereof) of an individual. The achievement of a whole (holy) relationship with all of life, healing is truly the province of religion.

These two realms, curing and healing, are not separate realms, but are rather a continuum with a shared boundary area. Here at the boundary are located the functional or psychosomatic ailments, those in which the body is made ill by the state of the mind or emotions. Likewise, here the mind is rendered less lucid by ills of the body. It is also in this area that the curative powers of the mind play a role in restoring the body's health, and the body's healthful trends clear the mind.

So we have four possibilities that may arise from the interplay between curing and healing. We may be both cured and healed, neither cured nor healed, cured but not healed, or healed but not cured.

Beset by incurable cancer, Judith Goodenough wrote a last letter to "neighbors and fellow creatures." In it she said

> I am writing from enormous pain and sickness and fever and fatigue. It does come to us sometimes to feel a change, a rearrangement in the

heart's geography, when we find that our longings face not the mornings but the evenings, when our thirsting is for sleep, rest, peace, and not for the golden beginnings of the day. This at least is what I have now, and at this gathering together the bad times are over for me, and there is no more pain, and there are no more tears.

Judith was healed, though not cured.
Come to think of it, we can be healed at any time that we devote mind and heart to the task. Curing is a sometime thing. Healing is an everyday possibility —even an ordinary day can be a graceful event.

GORDON B. McKEEMAN

SUNDAY MORNING

I declare a Sabbath Day—to walk in the wilderness of enlarged perceptions;

I declare a release from work—to nourish the stamina to pursue ideals;

I declare a special hour—to help cherish life's joys and combat life's sorrows;

I declare a reign of holiness—to deepen our grounding in the sustaining mystery.

I declare a time for simply being and letting go, for rediscovering great, forgotten truths, for basking in the arts of the ages, and for learning how to live again.

DAVID O. RANKIN

ABOUT THE AUTHORS

Kaaren Solveig Anderson is the minister at the Unitarian Universalist church in Utica, New York. She and her husband spend most of their free time changing diapers, playing violin, and singing "On Wisconsin!" with their three children whenever the need presents itself.

Jane Ellen Mauldin lives in Covington, Louisiana, with her husband, Harry Lowenburg; their children, Ben, Liz, and Sara; and their eager spaniel, Hanna. She has served as minister of the the Second Unitarian Church of Omaha, Nebraska; North Shore Unitarian Universalist Society of Louisiana; and Mobile Unitarian Universalist Congregation in Alabama. She is presently working full-time as a teacher for hospital- or homebound students.

Gordon B. McKeeman has been a Unitarian Universalist minister since 1943. He served as president of Starr King School for the Ministry for five years before his retirement in 1988. He currently lives in Charlottesville, Virgina, and enjoys working on needlepoint.

David O. Rankin has served as minister at Unitarian Universalist churches in San Francisco, California; Watertown and New Bedford, Massachusetts; and Atlanta, Georgia, as well as the independent Fountain Street Church in Grand Rapids, Michigan. He is now a freelance writer living in Moscow, Idaho, and he still uses a Smith Corona typewriter.

ALSO FROM SKINNER HOUSE BOOKS

Day of Promise: Collected Meditations, Volume One.
Collected by Kathleen Montgomery.
An anthology of one hundred meditations from more
than forty authors. ISBN 1-55896-419-3.

What We Share: Collected Meditations, Volume Two.
Collected by Patricia Frevert.
Meditations from Richard S. Gilbert, Bruce T. Marshall,
Elizabeth Tarbox, and Lynn Ungar. ISBN 1-55896-423-1.

All the Gifts of Life: Collected Meditations, Volume Three.
Collected by Patricia Frevert.
Meditations from Robert R. Walsh, Barbara Rohde, Gary
A. Kowalski, and Meg Barnhouse. ISBN 1-55896-437-1.

Listening for Our Song: Collected Meditations, Volume Four.
Collected by Margaret L. Beard.
Meditations from Jane Ranney Rzepka, David S. Blanchard,
Elizabeth Tarbox, and Sarah York. ISBN 1-55896-438-x.